How many apples are left?

A subtraction story.

How many apples are left?

A subtraction story

By: Ivelisse Marrero

About the author

I am the proud mother of twin boys Allen and William. At three years of age, they were diagnosed with autism, neurofibromatosis and an intellectual disability. Because of their disability and health conditions, they need individualized attention when it comes to their education. That's why I chose homeschooling. Through our homeschool journey, I have come to realize that they don't learn in the same way that other kids do. Therefore, I've had to come up with different teaching strategies to help them understand and process the world around them.

Growing up, I always enjoyed teaching others. At a very young age, I was working at a bookstore, and later on, I had the opportunity to work as a call center representative while studying biology at the University of Puerto Rico. A few years later, I decided that I wanted to become a pastry chef, so I enrolled in college one more time, gained experience doing this as a side hustle, and I was able to work as an Assistant Pastry Chef. When it was time for a new adventure, I left my native Puerto Rico and moved to the United States to become a flight attendant. This gave me the chance to be exposed to different cultures and to learn from people from all around the world.

Today, I am a full time homeschooling single-mom. Without a doubt, this has been the toughest, and yet, most rewarding job I've ever had.

About the book

When it comes to learning, we are all wired differently. It doesn't matter if we have a diagnosis of some sort, or a disability, or even if we are neurotypical. We all learn in different ways. Some people are more visual, some people are more hands-on, some learn through music, some learn by repetition, and the list goes on and on.

That's why I created this series. My goal is to share with the world the strategies that are working for us, so that anybody that has a child that struggles with learning a specific skill, can try them. I aim to tackle each skill with a different approach than the traditional one.

The purpose of this book is to learn subtraction in a different way. Kids can see how the tree has less and less apples as different characters take them away little by little. The story is also presented as a math equation so that learners can make the connection between the word and the standard form of the numbers.

I see an
apple tree
at the park.
How many apples
are on the tree?

There are 20 apples on the tree.

A girl took one apple from the tree. How many apples are left?

There are 19 apples left on the tree.
20 - 1 = 19

A boy
took two
apples from
the tree. How
many apples are left?

There are 17 apples left on the tree.
19 - 2 = 17

A squirrel
took one apple
from the tree. How
many apples are left?

There are 16 apples left on the tree.

17 - 1 = 16

A group
of birds took
three apples from
the tree. How many
apples are left?

There are 13 apples left on the tree.
16 - 3 = 13

A man took two apples from the tree. How many apples are left?

There
are 11
apples
left on
the tree.

13 - 2 = 11

A woman took one apple from the tree. How many apples are left?

There are 10 apples left on the tree.
11 - 1 = 10

A dog
took one
apple from
the tree. How

many apples are left?

There are 9 apples left on the tree.

10 - 1 = 9

A bear
took three
apples from
the tree. How
many apples are left?

There are 6 apples left on the tree.

9 - 3 = 6

A mouse
took one
apple from
the tree. How
many apples are left?

There are 5 apples left on the tree.

A rabbit
took two
apples from
the tree. How
many apples are left?

There are 3 apples left on the tree.

5 - 2 = 3

A horse
took two
apples from
the tree. How
many apples are left?

There is
1 apple
left on
the tree.
3 - 2 = 1

I took

one apple

from the tree. How

many apples are left?

There are 0 apples left on the tree.

1 - 1 = 0

THE

END